ARCO-AIRCAM AVIATION SERIES No. 6

Mk. IV, A29–629 'Cleopatra III' flown by Wing Commander G. C. Atherton, OC No. 80 Squadron, RAAF.

CURTISS KITTYHAWK MK I-IV
IN RAF·SAAF·RAAF·RNZAF·RCAF·NEIAF SERVICE

Illustrated & compiled by
Richard Ward

Text by
Christopher F. Shores

ACKNOWLEDGMENTS

Without the help of many friends this pictorial survey of the Kittyhawk, the first real fighter-bomber of the first Allied Tactical Air Force, the Desert Air Force, could not have been published. My thanks to all who helped whose names are listed below in alphabetical order:
A. Blake, Peter M. Bowers, R. A. Brown, d'E. C. Darby, J. F. Golding, Imperial War Museum, R. C. Jones, IPMS, G. H. Kamphuis, S. Kostenuk, W. B. Klepacki, D. W. Menard, B. Pattison, Eino Ritaranta, Frank F. Smith, R. Tester, Australian War Memorial, Royal Canadian Air Force, Royal New Zealand Air Force, South African Air Force, United States Navy.

Mk. IV, Royal Australian Air Force, A29–1193 in bare metal finish. black spinner, narrow OD anti glare panel

PUBLISHED BY

Arco Publishing Company, Inc., 219 Park Avenue South, New York, N.Y. 10003

First Published by Osprey Publications Ltd. and Printed in Great Britain

Library of Congress No. 75-93928 · Library Edition SBN 668-02104-7 · Paperback Edition SBN 668-02103-9

AIRCAM AVIATION SERIES Each publication illustrates one type or major sub-types of a famous aircraft in the colour schemes and markings of the Air Forces of the World. Each issue will contain eight pages of colour side view illustrations, supporting black and white plan view drawings showing where necessary both upper and under surfaces, one hundred and twenty-five half-tone photographs, each issue will also contain one full colour plate illustrating twenty examples of Unit Insignia of the World's Air Forces.

No. 1 **North American P-51D Mustang.** In USAAF-USAF service.

No. 2 **Republic P-47 Thunderbolt.** In USAAF–USAF; RAF; Free French; French Air Force; Mexican, Brazilian and other Air Forces.

No. 3 **North American Mustang Mk. I–IV.** In RAF; RAAF; SAAF; RNZAF; RCAF service and the **North American P-51B** and **D Mustang** in French; Italian; Swedish; Royal Netherlands; Netherlands East Indies; Indonesian; Israeli; Philippine; Dominican; Somali; South Korean; Chinese Nationalist; Chinese Communist, etc., Air Forces.

No. 4 **Supermarine Spitfire Mk. I–XVI, Merlin Engine.** In RAF; RAAF; SAAF; RCAF; USAAF; Belgian; Polish; Czechoslovakian; Free French; French; R. Norwegian; R. Netherlands; R. Danish; Israeli; Italian; Greek; Turkish; Portuguese; Egyptian; Burmese, etc., Air Forces.

No. 5 **North American P-51B/C Mustang.** In USAAF service. Similar content to No. 1 but with brief coverage of the P-51 and A-36.

No. 6 **Curtiss (P-40) Kittyhawk Mk. I–IV.** In RAF; RAAF; RNZAF; SAAF; RCAF; Netherlands East Indies; Russian and Finnish Air Forces. The Curtiss P-40 Warhawk will be covered in a future issue.

No. 7 **Curtiss P-40 Warhawk**

No. 8 **Supermarine Spitfire–Griffon Engine**

No. 9 **Spad Scouts**

No. 10 **Lockheed P-38 Lightning**

No. 11 **Consolidated B-24 Liberator**

No. 12 **Albatros Scouts**

No. 13 **Avro Lancaster**

No. 14 **Boeing B-17 Flying Fortress**

Aircam Special
Battle of Britain
The Supermarine Spitfire
Hawker Hurricane and
Messerschmitt Bf.109E.

Curtiss Kittyhawk Mk. I–IV

Training

Apart from its operational use, the Kittyhawk was employed in large numbers by the RAF in the Middle East, and by the SAAF, RCAF and RNZAF in the advanced training role.

Squadrons operating the Kittyhawk

RAF (and squadrons under RAF control), Middle East and Mediterranean area.

94, 112, 250, 260, 450, 3 RAAF, 2 SAAF, 4 SAAF and 5 SAAF Squadrons.

RAAF, South-West Pacific Area

75, 76, 77, 78, 80, 82, 84 and 86 Squadrons.

120 Squadron, Netherlands East Indies Air Force.

RNZAF, South Pacific Area

14, 15, 16, 17, 18, 19 and 20 Squadrons.

RCAF, Canada and Aleutians

14, 111, 118, 132, 133, 135 Squadrons.

Most successful Commonwealth Kittyhawk pilots in air combat

Middle East and Mediterranean Area

Sqn.Ldr. B. Drake 112 Squadron—15 victories
Fl.Lt. J. F. Edwards 260 Squadron—10½ victories a.l.
Sqn.Ldr. A. W. Barr 3 RAAF Squadron—9 victories
F.O. J. L. Waddy 250/260, 4 SAAF Squadron—8 victories

South-West Pacific Area

Wg.Cdr. L. D. Jackson 75, 80 Squadrons, RAAF and 78 Wing—5 victories
Wg.Cdr. G. C. Atherton 75, 82 and 80 Squadrons, RAAF and 78 Wing—5 victories

South Pacific Area

Wg.Cdr. P. G. H. Newton 17 Squadron, RNZAF—5 victories
F.O. G. B. Fisken 15 Squadron, RNZAF—5 victories

SPECIFICATION—CURTISS KITTYHAWK Mk. 1–IV

Type	Mk. I	Mk. Ia	Mk. III (P-40K)	Mk. III (P-40M)	Mk. IV
Span	37 ft. 4 in.	37 ft. 4 in.	37 ft. 4 in.	37 ft. 4 in.	37 ft. 4 in.
Length	31 ft. 2 in.	31 ft. 2 in.	31 ft. 2 in.	31 ft. 2 in.–33 ft. 4 in.	33 ft. 4 in.
Height	10 ft. 7 in.	10 ft. 7 in.	10 ft. 7 in.	10 ft. 7 in.	12 ft. 2 in.
Wing Area	236 sq. ft.	236 sq. ft.	236 sq. ft.	236 sq. ft.	236 sq. ft.
Weight empty	6208 lb.	6350 lb.	6400 lb.	6480 lb.	6000 lb.
Weight loaded	7740 lb.	8100/9100 lb.	8400 lb.	8000 lb.	7400 lb.
Weight loaded max.	8810 lb.	9200 lb.	10,000 lb.	8900 lb.	8850 lb.
Max. Speed at 15,000 ft.	350 m.p.h.	354 m.p.h.	362 m.p.h.	360 m.p.h.	343 m.p.h.
Range (miles)	800	700	700	700	750
Range max. (miles)	1150	1500	1600	1600	1400
Ceiling	30,600 ft.	29,000 ft.	28,000 ft.	30,000 ft.	30,000 ft.
Armament (all ·5 in. m.g's.)	4 or 6	6	6	6	4 or 6
Power unit	Allison V–1710–39 1150 h.p.	Allison V–1710–39 1150 h.p.	Allison V–1710–73 1325 h.p.	Allison V–1710–81 1200 h.p.	Allison V–1710–99 1200 h.p.

Front Cover - top to bottom

Mk. IV No. 120 Squadron, Netherlands East Indies Air Force, Merauke, Dutch New Guinea, 1944.
Mk. III No. 112 'Shark' Squadron, No. 239 Wing, Desert Air Force, RAF, 1943.
Mk. IV No. 15 Squadron, Royal New Zealand Air Force, flown by F.O. G. B. Fisken on Guadalcanal, summer 1943.
Mk. IV No. 76 Squadron, Royal Australian Air Force.
Mk. IV Serial 867, Royal Canadian Air Force.

With a desert warrior on the wing pointing the way a Kittyhawk Mk. III of No. 112 'Shark' Squadron taxies out from the dispersal area at LG 91, Amriyha. GA–F probably FR509

CURTISS KITTYHAWK MK.I-IV.

Early in 1940 Curtiss Aviation sought to improve the performance of the successful Hawk 81A, the P-40 Tomahawk, which had enjoyed substantial orders from both the U.S. and French governments, by the installation of a more powerful Allison V-1710-34 engine and an increased armament of four wing-mounted .50 in. machine guns. Some re-design of the nose of this new aircraft, the Hawk 87A, slightly altered the appearance, and the name was changed to Kittyhawk. In May the British government placed an order for 560 aircraft as the Kittyhawk Mark I, and when the first example was flown on 22 May, 1941, the aircraft was also ordered for the USAAF. It was as a result of an American requirement for increased armament that the aircraft was fitted with six .50 in. wing guns, and this modification was at once adopted by the British, 540 of the initial order being supplied in this configuration as the Mark IA. Early in 1941 substantial American orders were placed for the aircraft, including 1,500 Mark IAs for the RAF, purchased under Lease-Lend funds. In the event, 25 of these aircraft were delivered by surface transport to the RCAF, and others were sent to the Far East for use by the RAAF and RNZAF, following the Japanese attacks on Allied territories in December 1941. A number were also released by the RAF for delivery to Russia.

Apart from early test models, the majority of the RAF's Kittyhawks were delivered direct to the Middle East. As a result of the poor altitude performance of the Allison engines, efforts were made to install a Rolls Royce Merlin in the aircraft, and the next version to be produced, ordered for the USAAF as the P-40F, was fitted with a Packard-built Merlin V-1650-1. Most were used by the Americans, principally in the Middle East, but 250 were produced for Lease-Lend, 100 going to Russia, the rest being retained by the U.S. or supplied to the French (see later publication on the P-40 Warhawk). Known in the RAF as the Kittyhawk II, it has been stated that none of the aircraft went into service with this force, but in fact a few Mark IIs did find their way into Middle East squadrons during the summer of 1942.

Production of Allison-engined versions continued, the P-40K being the next production version, and a number of these were supplied to the RCAF late in 1942 for use in the Aleutians area, where the type was also employed by the USAAF. Twenty-one were shipped to the RAF as the Kittyhawk III, but these were soon followed by 595 P-40Ms, also known as Mark IIIs. This version was built solely for Lease-Lend, all but five being allotted initially to the RAF, some serving in the Middle East, though the majority were shipped to the Far East and to Russia. Though built solely for Lease-Lend a few found their way into the USAAF.

The final production version was the P-40N, produced as a lightened edition of the aircraft. It was built in larger numbers than any of the earlier models, and 586 of the main production model, with a revised cockpit canopy, were supplied to the RAF as the Mark IV, serving in Italy, and with the Australians, New Zealanders and Dutch in the Far East. Large numbers were also supplied to Russia, this nation receiving a total of 2,097 P-40s during the war (although a small percentage of these were the earlier Tomahawks).

The Kittyhawk in service with the R.A.F.

First unit in the Middle East to receive Kittyhawks was 3 RAAF Squadron, exchanging Tomahawks for these aircraft during December 1941 and beginning operations from Msus on 27th of that month; 112 Squadron withdrew to similarly re-equip before the turn of the year. Employed during the first part of 1942 as the RAF's main air superiority fighter, the first Kittyhawk combats were fought by the Australians on New Year's Day, when they claimed four Ju 87s and a Bf 109 destroyed, one of each probably destroyed and four damaged for the loss of their commanding officer. The tables were turned eight days later, when 112 Squadron joined 3 RAAF at the front. On one mission the Australians were bounced by Bf 109s, losing two of their number, and later in the day an aircraft of 112 Squadron was also shot down; no claims were made by the Commonwealth pilots. At the end of the month a new squadron joined operations for the first time, this being 450 (Australian) Squadron, also flying Kittyhawks.

During the early months of 1942 the Kittyhawks flew fighter sweeps, bomber escorts and interception missions, frequently taking heavy toll of Axis dive-bombers and Italian fighters. However, though rugged and manoeuvreable, the aircraft was out-performed by the darting Messerschmitt Bf 109Fs, which used their better altitude performance to sit above the British fighters, making diving attacks and climbing away, avoiding dog-fights whenever possible. Throughout the campaign these formid-

Above AK571 the first Kittyhawk Mk. I Green/brown and pale blue scheme. *(Photo IWM)*

Above & Centre Mk. I in sand and stone camouflage. Note two guns, nose and cockpit details. *(Photo IWM)*

able aircraft, piloted by a handful of highly-experienced pilots, took a regular toll of the Kittyhawks, on occasions shooting down four or five aircraft from one squadron in a single mission.

Typical of these operations were those on 14 and 15 February, 1942. On the former day, eight Kittyhawks of 3 RAAF Squadron and 10 of 112 Squadron engaged 32 Axis aircraft, claiming 20 destroyed without loss. Nearly every pilot engaged put forward a claim, the Australians claiming four Bf 109s, 3½ Macchi 200s and a Macchi 202, while 112 Squadron claimed 10½ Macchi 200s and a Bf 109. Several claims for probables and damaged were also made. Next day 112 Squadron lost two aircraft to Lt. Hans-Joachim Marseille of I/JG 27 in the morning, and in the afternoon 12 aircraft from this squadron, accompanied by eight from 94 Squadron set off to strafe Martuba landing ground. 94 Squadron had just received their Kittyhawks, having taken very heavy losses earlier in the campaign when flying Hurricanes, and this was their first mission, led by a new commanding officer, Sqn.-Ldr. E. M. 'Imshi' Mason, who had been top-scoring RAF fighter pilot of the First Libyan Campaign a year earlier. One Bf 109, flown by Ofw. Otto Schulz of II/JG 27 managed to get off the ground to intercept the attack, but this lone pilot shot down and killed Mason and three N.C.O. pilots of 94 Squadron, and badly damaged one of 112's aircraft. 94 Squadron was at once withdrawn for further training.

On 8 March a dozen Kittyhawks from 450 and 3 RAAF Squadrons intercepted 15 Ju 87s, nine Macchis and two Bf 109s over Tobruk, the Italians mistaking the Australians for friendly aircraft with disastrous results; seven Macchis and two Ju 87s were claimed shot down. 112 Squadron on a sweep met the scattered remnants of the formation, claiming another two. Two days later, the commander of the latter unit, Sqn.-Ldr. C. R. Caldwell, test-dropped a 250 lb. bomb — a sign of things to come.

During March another Kittyhawk unit, 260 Squadron, began operations, and on 21st 94 Squadron was called back into action, immediately losing one aircraft. In mid-April 250 Squadron also arrived at the front with Kittyhawks, but early in May 94 Squadron was ordered to hand all aircraft to 2 SAAF Squadron, to replace that unit's Tomahawks and to withdraw to fly Hurricanes on rear area defence duties. The more experienced pilots were posted to 260 Squadron.

On 12 May, 1942, Kittyhawks from 250 Squadron escorted Beaufighters of 252 Squadron to intercept a formation of Ju 52s crossing the Mediterranean, the first time such a mission had been attempted. A formation, reported as 16 Ju 52s and two Bf 110s, was sighted, and the British aircraft carried out a devasting frontal attack, before sweeping round to catch the survivors. Claims from the Kittyhawks totalled 10 Ju 52s and two Bf 110s, F.O. J. L. Waddy alone claiming four aircraft, while the Beaufighters claimed another five Ju 52s. Subsequent research shows that the formation actually consisted of 14 Ju 52s and one Bf 110, but nonetheless 10 aircraft were lost and others damaged.

On 16 May 112 Squadron began operations as the first Kittybomber unit, and the following month, during the great Gazala battles, the first Spitfires appeared overhead, altering the Kittyhawks' role. Throughout June and July many fighter-bomber and strafing missions were flown in an effort to stop the Axis advance, and losses to ground-fire were heavy. At the height of these operations, 4 SAAF Squadron also began replacing their Tomahawks with Kittyhawks, operating a mixed complement of both types for some weeks.

After the 8th Army's consolidation on the Alamein Line, the two Kittyhawk Wings, 239, composed of 112, 250, 450 and 3 RAAF Squadrons, and 233, composed of 260, 2 SAAF, 4 SAAF and 5 SAAF (still flying Tomahawks) Squadrons, settled down to a steady routine of bomber escort missions, the former Wing usually accompanying the Baltimore squadrons while the latter looked after the Bostons. The squadrons frequently carried bombs on these missions, going down to ground level after the main attack to ferret out anything missed by the mediums. The escort provided by these squadrons was extremely effective, and bomber losses to Axis fighters were very light, though the losses suffered by their charges were frequently substantial.

During the Battle of El Alamein the Kittyhawk again took part in a fair amount of strafing and ground attack work in addition to their escort duties, now joined by the P-40 squadrons of the growing U.S. 9th Air Force. With the advance towards Tripoli and the Tunisian border, nearly all Hurricane units were left behind, and the Kittyhawk became the main ground-support aircraft of the Desert Air Force, supporting the Army in this role with considerable effect during the Mareth and Wadi Zigzau battles. That the Axis fighters had teeth in Tunisian skies was proved to 112 Squadron on 10 March, 1943. Bounced by a mixed force of the enemy, the squadron claimed three to take their total for the war to over 200, but in so doing, lost six aircraft and pilots.

5 SAAF Squadron, the last Tomahawk unit, was finally re-equipped early in 1943, though many pilots preferred the greater sensitivity of control of the earlier aircraft. During April 1943 USAAF aircraft on several occasions inflicted heavy losses on large formations of German transport aircraft in the Cap Bon area, as these attempted to supply the Axis forces in Tunisia. On 19 April the SAAF Kittyhawks had their turn, 2 SAAF Squadron claiming five Ju 52s, two SM 82s and a probable, while 5 SAAF Squadron claimed 8 Ju 52s and two probables, a Re 2001 and a Ju 87 together with a glider it was towing. Three days later 4 and 5 SAAF Squadrons met a formation of six-engined Me 323s and claimed an even bigger victory, nine being credited to the former unit and 13-15 to the latter.

When the campaign in North Africa ended in May 1943, the Kittyhawk squadrons had, since 1 January, 1942, claimed over 420 enemy aircraft shot down in combat, with others claimed as probables or damaged, and had also destroyed many more on the ground. Most successful unit in air combat was 112 Squadron with 79 victories while flying Kittyhawks, and many of the leading pilots in the Desert had gained some of their successes on this type, including Sqn.-Ldr. C. R. Caldwell and Sqn.-Ldr. B. Drake of 112 Squadron, F.O. J. L. Waddy of 250 Squadron, Sqn.-Ldrs. R. W. Gibbes and A. W. Barr of 3 RAAF Squadron, and Fl.-Lt. J. F. Edwards of 260 Squadron.

After the final surrender of the Axis in Africa, the Kittyhawks' main task was more than ever to be ground support. By the time the invasion of Sicily took place, 2 and 4 SAAF Squadrons had converted to Spitfire Vs, but all other Kittyhawk squadrons took part in this campaign and in the subsequent invasion of Italy. During this period there was little opportunity for air combat, and in fact only a few more victories were to be claimed by 112 and 3 RAAF Squadrons during late 1943 and early 1944. The last combat occurred on 7 April, 1944, when 12 Kittyhawks of 112 surprised 12 Fw 190s taking off from Rieti and shot down three for the loss of two. Carrying 500 lb. bombs, close support of a very high standard was afforded to the armies advancing up the Italian mainland, and though 112, 260 and 3 RAAF Squadrons gave up their Kittyhawk IVs, and 5 SAAF Squadron their Kittyhawk IIIs for the more modern Mustang IIs during the latter part of 1944, 250 and 450 Squadrons soldiered on with their Mark IVs until after the final surrender in May 1945, finally handing their aircraft in to depots during the late summer.

With the R.A.A.F.

With the rapid Japanese advance early in 1942, the Australian homeland came in imminent danger of invasion, and in February 1942, 25 Kittyhawk IAs, released from the RAF's initial contract for the type, arrived, being formed during March into 75 Squadron around a small nucleus of experienced pilots withdrawn from the Middle East. On 21 March the squadron flew to Port Moresby to provide air cover to this port on the south coast of New Guinea, leaving the defence of Darwin and the North-Western Territories to American P-40s of the 49th Fighter Group.

The day of arrival, the squadron was in the air intercepting a raid and claiming their first victory, and next day they carried the war to the enemy, strafing Lae airfield on the North side of the island. The Kittyhawks were intercepted by the already-notorious Mitsubishi A6M Zero-Sens, losing two of their number, but claiming two Zeros shot down. By the end of the first three days seven of the 17 Kittyhawks had been lost to one cause or another. During April the squadron escorted USAAF A-24 Dauntlesses over Lae, being involved in several fierce fights with Zeros with losses on both sides. On 28 April the commanding officer, Sqn.-Ldr. J. Jackson, led the last five serviceable aircraft against a raid by escorted bombers, but both he and another pilot were shot down and killed, while a third aircraft was damaged. Two days later two squadrons of P-39s of the U.S. 8th Fighter Group arrived to relieve the Australians, but for several more days such aircraft as could be got into the air accompanied these on missions until on 9 May only one aircraft was fit to fly back to the mainland, a second following two days later. In 44 days of combat the squadron had shot down 18 aircraft and destroyed 17 on the ground, claiming four more probably destroyed and 47 damaged for a loss of 22 Kittyhawks of 31 received, nine in combat, four missing, three on the ground and six in accidents; 12 pilots were killed or missing. Sqn.-Ldr. L. Jackson, who had taken over after his brother's death, had shot down four aircraft and F.O. Piper 3½.

Meanwhile two more squadrons had been formed, these being Nos. 76 and 77. On 25 July, 75 and 76 Squadrons flew to Milne Bay, New Guinea, an area in danger of invasion. The first combat occurred on 4 August when eight aircraft of 76 Squadron intercepted a raid, Fl.-Lt. Ash shooting down a dive-bomber, but on 11th 22 Kittyhawks from both squadrons intercepted 12 Zeros, losing four Kittyhawks for a claim of four Zeros probably shot down. On 24th an invasion fleet appeared and landings began, both squadrons at once beginning a series of almost continuous strafing and bombing attacks on the Japanese troops and vessels. Occasional air attacks were met, and on 27th four dive-bombers and two Zeros were shot down, but on this day the commander of 76 Squadron, Sqn.-Ldr. P. Turnbull, a veteran of the Desert, crashed and was killed while strafing. On 6 September, mainly due to heavy losses inflicted by air attack, the Japanese withdrew, never to return, and next day the Kittyhawks escorted the first offensive mission flown by Australian Beauforts and Beaufighters. The action of the Kittyhawks during the invasion was summed up by the Australian commander, General Blamey, in the words: "The action of 75 and 76 Squadrons, RAAF, on the first

Mk. I, GA–V flown by P/O N. Duke, serial unknown, photographs probably taken at Gambut Main, Libya, April 1942. *(Credit unknown)*

day was probably the decisive factor." On 21 September the squadrons were again relieved by U.S. 8th Fighter Group P-39s, 75 Squadron then flying to Horn Island and 76 Squadron to the North-West area.

Here the latter unit was joined by 77 Squadron which had been based in Western Australia since formation, and these units took over the defence of the Darwin area from the U.S. P-40s later in the year. No daylight raids materialized during this period, but attempts were made to intercept night bombers, culminating on 23 November when Sqn.-Ldr. Cresswell, commander of 77 Squadron, shot one down. Early in 1943 the squadrons were relieved by the newly-arrived Spitfires of 1 Fighter Wing, and 77 Squadron then flew to Milne Bay where they were joined by 75 Squadron.

At this time a limited offensive was beginning, the Japanese advance having been held, and the squadrons carried out escort missions to Beauforts until May, when 77 moved to Goodenough Island with 76 and 79 (Spitfire) Squadrons to cover landings on the north coast of New Guinea during June, 75 Squadron also taking part from Milne Bay. Attacks by Beauforts, Beaufighters and Bostons on Gasmata and Rabaul were escorted from these bases.

New Kittyhawk squadrons were still being formed, and in July 86 Squadron flew to Merawke for air defence, and the following month 78 Squadron joined the others on Goodenough Island, moving forward to Kiriwina with 76 and 79 Squadrons as 71 Wing, to take part in the Lae-Nadzab and Finschafen operations. Towards the end of the year 75, 76, 77 and 78 Squadrons, grouped as 73 Wing, all took part in a series of assaults on Rabaul, Gasmata and the Bismarks, these coinciding with attacks by the U.S. 13th Air Force from the Solomons which included R.N.Z.A.F. Kittyhawk squadrons in its strength. During this period many bomber escort missions were flown, together with dive-bombing attacks.

During January 1944 86 Squadron at Merawke at last saw some action. On 22nd, two Kittyhawks patrolled over Cape Valsch after a regular Japanese reconnaissance aircraft, this being duly intercepted and shot down. Next day two more fighters saw a 'Betty' and an escorting 'Zeke', Fl.-Lt. Whittle shooting down the latter and then sharing with Fl.-Sgt. Kerrison in destroying the bomber. The Japanese did not come again. 86 Squadron shared the defence of the area with 84 Squadron which had exchanged Boomerangs for Kittyhawks the previous October.

At the turn of the year a new Group was formed on New Guinea and this included a new Kittyhawk Wing, No. 78, made up of 75, 78 and 80 Squadrons, which went into action in January, strafing and bombing targets in Northern New Guinea, and escorting Mitchells and R.A.A.F. Vengeances. On 3 June patrolling Kittyhawks of 78 Squadron from this Wing met 12 'Oscars' and three 'Kates' over Biak, and in a 40 minutes dogfight, shot down seven of the fighters and two bombers for the loss of one Kittyhawk. Seven days later eight aircraft from the same squadron, while covering a convoy, saw an enemy aircraft, and this was shot down in flames by two of them, the last R.A.A.F. victory in the New Guinea theatre, and the last claimed by an Australian Kittyhawk.

During the summer reforms were made in the organisation of squadrons, and when, in September, a second Wing, No. 81, was formed with 76, 77 and 82 Squadrons, 84 and 86 Squadrons, still on home defence duties, were disbanded to increase the capacity of the other units. Following an assault by U.S. forces, in which 78 Wing was heavily involved, both Wings moved up to Noemfoor and Morotai, and late in the year 1st Tactical Air Force was formed at the former base, incorporating both Wings under the command of Air-Cdr. A. H. Cobby, a famous 'ace' of the First War.

When the Americans began their assault on the Philippines the R.A.A.F. units and the U.S. 13th Air Force operated only in a supporting role, 5th Air Force giving immediate cover to the landings. The Australians were involved in neutralizing surrounding islands, notably Halmahera, suffering considerable losses to ground fire in the process. It now became obvious that the Australians were not to be invited forward to the new bases, and for the rest of the war they were involved in holding operations against by-passed garrisons which were steadily neutralized and mopped-up. These operations included attacks on Celebes in February 1945, the occupation of Tarakan in the spring, the Labuan and Brunei operations, where aircraft of 81 Wing managed to destroy one or two aircraft on the ground, and finally in June and July, operations over the former Dutch territories in the East Indies. All these involved mainly ground support missions. Just as the war came to a close the first P-51D Mustangs arrived, and these soon replaced the Kittyhawks in all squadrons.

With the R.N.Z.A.F.

In December 1941, following requests to Britain for reinforcements, 142 Kittyhawk IAs were released for the R.A.A.F. and R.N.Z.A.F., the latter force receiving 18 in spring 1942, these providing the basis of 14 Squadron with a nucleus of pilots from 488 Squadron who had lost their aircraft in the retreat from the East Indies. Eighty more Kittyhawks were allocated to the R.N.Z.A.F., and by June 44 of these had arrived, 15 and 16 Squadrons being formed, followed in October by 17 Squadron. In this month the first fighter pilots were sent overseas, 15 Squadron taking over 23 American P-40s in poor condition from the U.S. 68th Fighter Squadron at Santo, for air defence duties.

In April 1943 14 Squadron flew their own Kittyhawks to Santo, and these were then taken on to Guadalcanal by 15 Squadron, where, suitably daubed with white recognition bands, the squadron began operations on 29 April, flying with U.S. P-38s and P-40s and Navy and Marine SBDs, TBFs, F4Us and F4Fs. On 7 June, 1943, 40—50 Japanese fighters were met between Buraku and the Russells, when Allied fighters were escorting dive-bombers. Twenty-three were claimed, four by 12 Kittyhawks of 15 Squadron in their first combat, no loss being suffered by the New Zealanders.

The first R.N.Z.A.F. Kittyhawk was lost on 12 June when 14 Squadron, arriving to relieve 15, scrambled and shot down six enemy aircraft for the loss of one. This

Above, Centre & Right
Neat formations by four replacement aircraft of No. 112 'Shark' Squadron, note all aircraft have Azure blue under surfaces. *(All photos IWM)*

Below
AK772 (nearest a/c in all three photos above) complete with 'Sharkmouth' and code. 'London Pride' in small white script above Y. Note extended fuse on 250 lb bomb. Gambut, 1942. *(IWM)*

GA–C taxying out to the field with billowing clouds of dust being whipped up by the airscrew, typical operating conditions on Desert Landing Grounds. LG 91, Amriyha, Egypt, 1942. *(Photos IWM)*

squadron was then involved in patrols over Rendova, claiming seven for the loss of two Kittyhawks on 1 July and five for on 3rd, three of these being credited to F.O. G. B. Fisken. One Kittyhawk crash-landed and one was damaged. On 25 July the squadron was relieved by 16 Squadron which had arrived at Santo in June, and then flew back to New Zealand for a rest, having claimed 22 shot down and four probables for the loss of four aircraft and three pilots. 17 Squadron now also flew out to Santo, a further squadron, 18, having been formed in June.

No. 16 Squadron flew their first major mission on 31 July, escorting SBDs and TBFs to Munda, but were bounced by 30 Zeros, and two Kittyhawks were shot down. The squadron was relieved in mid-September by 17 Squadron, and also returned to New Zealand for a rest. The R.N.Z.A.F. pilots had made a good name for themselves with the U.S. bomber crews and were much sought after for close escort. A U.S. request was now made for increased representation and 15 Squadron joined 17 at Guadalcanal to form the R.N.Z.A.F. Fighter Wing, while 18 Squadron flew to Santo. On 1 October off Vella Lavella Japanese dive-bombers attacked a convoy carrying New Zealand troops, being intercepted by eight Kittyhawks of 15 Squadron and 12 U.S. F4Us, the New Zealanders claiming seven of the 'Vals'.

Late in October the squadrons moved forward to Ondonga on New Georgia to help cover landings on Bougainville and as these went in on 1 November 18 Squadron attacked 50—60 'Zekes', claiming seven and a probable for the loss of one aircraft. During the month over 1,000 sorties were made by the Wing and for the first time strafing attacks were laid on. During December sweeps began against Rabaul, refuelling at Torokina on Bougainville. 14 and 16 Squadrons relieved 15 and 18, and were in turn relieved by 17, and then 15 again in late December. In a fight on 17 December the New Zealanders shot down five aircraft but lost two, including the Wing Leader, Wg.-Cdr. Freeman. On 24 December while on a sweep with U.S. fighters, they met 40+ Japanese fighters and gained their best score to date, claiming 12 destroyed and four probables for the loss of five Kittyhawks.

In January 15 and 17 Squadrons moved up to Torokina to continue their close escort to U.S. bombers over Rabaul, where Japanese fighter opposition remained heavy. During the last 10 days of January 1944 the New Zealanders fought six battles, claiming eight 'Zekes' for the loss of three Kittyhawks, and on 22nd 18 Squadron replaced 17, the latter returning home. On 13 February, while escorting TBFs to Vunakanau airfield, this former squadron met 25 'Zekes', shooting down two for the loss of one. These victories brought the total claims of the R.N.Z.A.F. Kittyhawks to 99 shot down and were the last they were to gain, as on 19th the Japanese withdrew their fighters from the area, having decided that their further use was uneconomical.

During their ten months in combat, two New Zealand pilots had each shot down five Japanese aircraft, these being Sqn.-Ldr. P. Newton of 17 Squadron and F.O. G. B. Fisken of 15 Squadron; Fisken had previously shot down six aircraft in Burma and was probably the top-scoring Commonwealth pilot against the Japanese.

Two further squadrons had been formed, 19 in December 1943 and 20 in January 1944, and the former moved to Torokina in March to relieve 18 Squadron. In this month the R.N.Z.A.F. squadrons really began fighter-bomber and dive-bombing attacks, initially carrying 500 lb. bombs, but from 21 March 1,000 pounders were frequently carried. Attacks were made on Rabaul and targets on Bougainville, but in May the first Corsairs arrived for the R.N.Z.A.F., and during the year all the Kittyhawks were replaced by these.

With the R.C.A.F.

Twenty-five Kittyhawks were supplied to the R.C.A.F. in March 1942, followed by more later, and six home defence squadrons of Western Air Command were equipped with these aircraft, the first squadron being despatched at once to assist the U.S. forces in Alaska and the Aleutians, where for several months patrolling and strafing missions were flown. On 25 September, 1942, 11 Kittyhawks of 14 and 111 Squadrons accompanied six U.S. P-40s and 11 P-39s to strafe the Japanese base on Kiska. During this mission two 'Rufe' floatplane fighters were shot down, one by Sqn.-Ldr. K. A. Boomer of 111 Squadron, this being the only victory of the war gained by R.C.A.F. home-based units. Canadian Kittyhawks remained in the area until the Japanese withdrew from Kiska in August 1943, when they returned to Canada.

With the Netherlands East Indies Air Force

Pilots of the Netherlands East Indies Air Force who escaped to Australia in 1942 formed several squadrons, operating under R.A.A.F. command, and one of these, 120 Squadron, was formed during 1943 with Kittyhawks. The unit initially served on home defence duties in the North-Western Territories, but in mid 1945 took part in operations over the East Indies in company with Australian Kittyhawk units, flying strafing and bombing missions. After the war, the squadron was based on Java, flying alongside Dutch Mustang units, and took part in several actions against Indonesian nationalist guerillas, the last known operational missions flown by Curtiss aircraft. In 1949 the squadron was just beginning to re-equip with Mustangs when the Dutch moved out of Indonesia, and all remaining aircraft were handed to the new Republic. The subsequent fate of the remaining aircraft is uncertain.

With the Russians

Some 2,000 Kittyhawks of various models were supplied to the Soviet Union, but little is known of their use by this country. Certainly, unlike the British and Americans, the Russians did not prefer them to the Bell P-39 Airacobra, considering that they did not absorb battle damage as well as the latter, or have the same punch with regard to armament. It is believed that many were used for advanced training, but some were supplied to the Soviet Navy and flown on the North Russian front. The Safonov unit, which had previously flown I-16s, MiG 3s and Hurricanes, operated these aircraft for some time, and several pilots gained a number of successes with the Kittyhawks, including Senior Lt. Nikolai Fedorovich Kuznetsov, who ended the war with 36 victories.

At least one Russian Kittyhawk was captured intact by Finnish forces, and this, coded KH-51, was issued to Finnish fighter squadron HLeLv 32, to operate alongside the unit's Curtiss Hawk 75As, and three captured LaGG 3s, joining the latter in the high speed, low level reconnaissance role.

Bomb rack details, 250 lb with extended fuse.

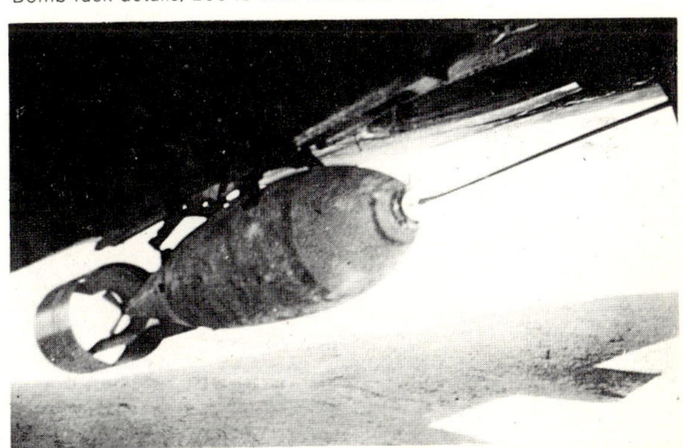

Above Mk. Ia taxying out of the rough at Sidi Heneish, Egypt, April 1942.

Above GA–C, ET789 forced landed in the desert near Daba after destroying a Ju. 87D and Bf.109E. Flown by Sgt. Hogg, SAAF. *(IWM)*

Below GA–M, FR864, note 2 x 250 lb side by side under fuselage and 4 x 40 lb bombs under wings. *(IWM)*

Right Mk. Ia, AK772, GA–Y of No. 112 'Shark' Squadron. Appears to have 2 x 250 lb bombs mounted in tandem under fuselage, an arrangement also used by the 23rd Fighter Group, USAAF, with both bombs and long range tanks. Gambut, Libya, June 1942.

A few words about the origin of the Sharkmouth insignia sported by No. 112 Squadron may not be out of place here. Contrary to what has appeared in print elsewhere, No. 112 Sqdn. originated this marking so far as Allied use is concerned, it was, of course, copied from the Messerschmitt Bf.110's of ZG76, who No. 112 Sqdn., at the time flying Gladiators, fought over Greece and Crete in 1941. The remnants of the squadron on their return to Egypt were reformed and re-equipped with the Tomahawk conversion taking place at Feyid in the Canal Zone during July 1941. First ops. were flown from Sidi Barrani and Sidi Heneish during August and during the following month, September, the 'Sharkmouth' appeared an A Flight aircraft at Sidi Heneish. The squadron was visited by the press in late September or early October and the resulting photographs were released for general publication, a two page spread appearing in the Illustrated London News, a copy of which found its way to Rangoon where at the time one squadron of the American Volunteer Group, were stationed and the rest is history. Who was responsible for the first 112 'Sharkmouth' is not known for sure though a certain Pilot Officer Westenra may have been the originator.

Above left Mk. Ia, AK673 No. 112 Squadron, on strength Jan. 42, El Adem, off Feb. Gambut Main.
(R. Tester via R. C. Jones)

Above, right Poor photograph but interesting, a Mk. III of No. 112 Squadron with USAAF serial on rudder, 245798. Medenine/El Hamma March/April 1943. *(SAAF)*

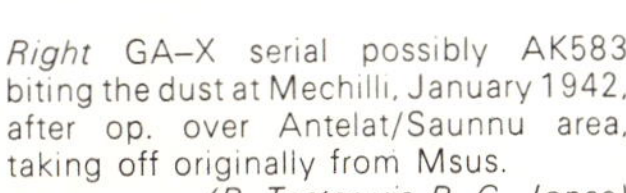

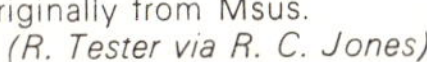

Right GA–X serial possibly AK583 biting the dust at Mechilli, January 1942, after op. over Antelat/Saunnu area, taking off originally from Msus.
(R. Tester via R. C. Jones)

Line-up of No. 112 Squadron Mk. Ia's at Sidi Heneish, 14th April 1942. *(R. A. Brown)*

GA–A, serial unknown, probably on LG 106, El Daba, Egypt, Nov. 1942. Note yellow outer ring in under wing roundel and Azure blue under surfaces.

Right Mk. III, FR302, GA–T probably on Martuba 4, Libya, November 1942.

Below Mk. III, serial unknown, GA–C probably on Antelat LG, Libya. *(IWM)*

Above Four Mk. III's of No. 112 Squadron, note three a/c with 'Sharkmouths' carry 2 x 250 lb bombs. *(IWM)*

Above Mk. III's touching down at Zuarz, Tripolitania, April 1943. *(via R. A. Brown)*

Right Sqdn.Ldr. P. F. Illingworth, O.C. No. 112 Squadron 15.7.43–29.3.44

Below Mk. IV, GA–? FX740 taking off from Cutella, Italy. Note bomb load, 1 x 500 lb under fuselage, 2 x 250 lb under wings. Flt.Lt. Ross

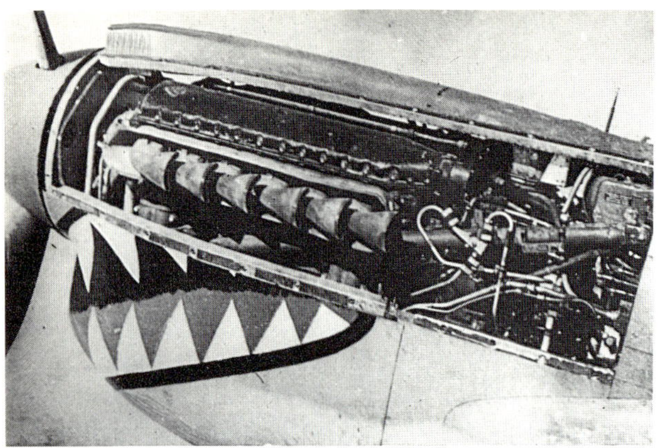

Allison engine detail.

Damaged radio compartment of FR474, GA–Jinx after combat with Fe.190's over Rieti LG, Italy, 7th April 1944. Flown by Flt.Lt. Matthias, No. 112 Squadron.

Detail shot showing wing guns, camera gun and bomb rack.

GA–B, FT854 damaged in combat over Rieti LG *(All photos via R. A. Brow*

A complete rudder and the remains brought back by Flt.Lt. Bluett from a strafing op. No. 112 Squadron.

GA–D, FR860 damaged by flak over Messina. No. 112 Squadron.

Above Line-up of No. 112 'Shark' Squadron and No. 260 Squadron at Pachino LG, note two Kittyhawks lining up for take-off. *(via R. A. Brown)*

Above GA–Q, FR806, USAAF OD and grey scheme. Note 2 x 250 lb bombs under fuselage and 6 x 40 lb under wings. Foggia Main, Italy. *(via R. A. Brown)*

Below Mk. IV bombed up with 3 x 250 lb bombs taxying out for take-off on an airfield in Italy. No. 112 Squadron. *(IWM)*

Right Line-up of 'Sharkmouths', note nearest aircraft has odd panels. Brindisi LG, September 1943. *(IWM)*

Below Line-up of No. 260 Squadron Kittyhawks on a desert landing ground, no doubt after the press photographs had been duly taken the squadron dispersed over the usual two to three miles occupied by a desert squadron. *(IWM)*

ve Same line-up as on facing page, note
w outer ring to under wing roundel on
blue under surfaces. *(IWM)*

Plan view detail shot, note camera gun
ng on starboard wing.

v Nose detail of a Mk. III, note full span
w leading edge stripe, wing racks and
e blue under surfaces. *(IWM)*

Above Mk. I flown by Sqdn. Ldr. M. T. Judd, CO of No. 250 'Sudan' Squadron, Western Desert, August 1942. *(IWM)*

Below A pair of No. 250 Squadron Mk. III's taking off from a landing ground in Italy. *(IWM)*

Below FR241 revving up prior to take-off, note yellow outer ring to under wing roundel on Azure blue under surfaces. LD–R of No. 250 Squadron. *(IWM)*

cal Western Desert scene,
hawks loosely lined-up await-
ake-off time.
shot shows aircraft of No. 260
dron, HS– nearest camera
No. 5 SAAF, GL– in distance.
er shot shows No. 2 SAAF
dron, all squadrons of No. 233
, RAF, Desert Air Force.
(Photos IWM)

Above Mk. Ia flown by Major D. B. Hauptfliesch, AFC, CO No. 2 SAAF Squadron, photo probably taken on one of the Amriyha landing grounds. Serial unknown. *(via A. Blake)*

Mk. III flown by Maj. Hauptfliesch, CO No. 2 SAAF Squadron. *(SAAF via A. Blake)*

Below 'Lady Godiva' a Mk. III of No. 5 SAAF Squadron on an airfield in Italy. Note red/white quartered wheel disc and yellow leading edge stripe to u/c fairing. *(IWM)*

Below Mk. IV of an OTU in South Africa, see colour illustration. *(SAAF)*

Above Bombed up Mk. Ia's of No. 3 RAAF Squadron on a desert landing ground. *(Australian War Memorial)*

Below Mk. Ia's of Nos. 3 and 450 RAAF Squadrons taxying out for take-off on bombing op. *(Australian War Memorial)*

Above and below Line-up of No. 3 RAAF Kittyhawks. Note CV–U in USAAF desert pink scheme but with Azure blue under surfaces, white star on red wheel disc. All a/c with full span yellow leading edge stripes. *(Photos IWM)*

Left Mk. III, No. 3 RAAF Squadron, Zua
Tripolitania, 1943. See colour illustration
port side details. *(via R. C. Jones)*

Right AK581, CV–J No. 3 RAAF Squadron down in the desert somewhere in 1941. Note large J. *(via Frank F. Smith)*

Below Mk. III's of No. 450 RAAF Squadron on an airfield on Malta. *(AWM)*

Left Kittyhawks of No. 450 RA
Squadron taxying out to the runw
San Angelo, Italy, 1944.
(via R. C. Jon

ve Kittyhawks of either No. 75 or 76
n. at Milne Bay, New Guinea, July
2. Green/brown uppers, pale blue
ers. Red/white/blue roundels and
flash. *(IWM)*

ot Mk. Ia, A29–96 of No. 75 Sqdn.
F at Milne Bay 1942. IU was 75's
e at this time subsequently changed
A. 'U–Bute' on cowl, green/brown
ers, pale blue unders. A29–45
ers Revenge' in distance. *(AWM)*

ve Mk. Ia coded IF of No. 76
adron, Milne Bay. Note red/white/
roundels. *(AWM)*

ot Sqdn.Ldr. K. W. 'Bluey' Truscott
No. 76 Squadron, taxying in A29–142
Milne Bay. Note wavy finish to
ouflage, serial in grey. *(AWM)*

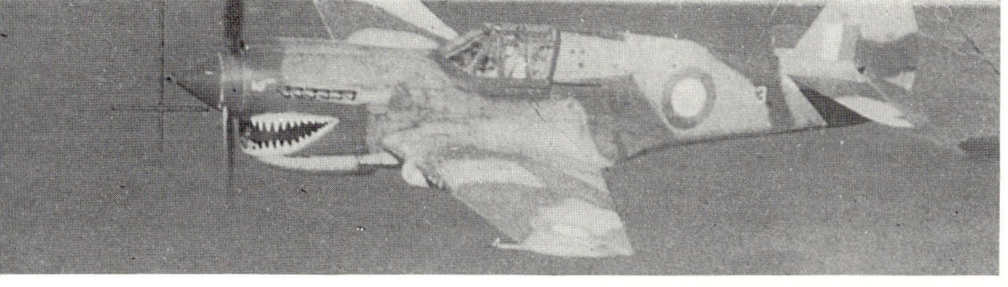

ove 'Sharkmouthed' Mk. Ia, A29–83 of No. 1
U, East Sale, Victoria, see colour illustration.
(via Frank F. Smith)

ht Mk. Ia, A29–310 of No. 2 OTU, Mildura,
w South Wales. *(via Frank F. Smith)*

Above Mk. Ia, A29–130 of the Central Gunnery School, Cressy, Victoria. Green/brown uppers, pale blue unders. *(via Frank P. Smith)*

Above (3 pictures) Mk. Ia, A29–144 of the Central Gunnery School, Cressy, Victoria, after a forced landing sometime in 1944. Green/brown uppers, pale blue unders. Note A29 only on stbd. side, 144 only on port side in grey, 44 in white. *(via Frank F. Smith)*

Right Mk. III, No. 2 OTU, Mildura, 1944. Bare metal and OD scheme. *(via Frank F. Smith)*

Left Mk. IV of No. 75 Squadron, RAA[illegible] collapsed undercart probably due to burs[illegible] Serial probably A29–1019 *(via Frank F. [illegible]*

1
Mk. I, No. 250 'Sudan' Squadron, No. 239 Wing, RAF, Desert Air Force, 1942. Flown by Sqdn.-Ldr. M. T. Judd, Squadron OC. AK919.

2
Mk. I, No. 250 'Sudan' Squadron, No. 239 Wing, RAF, Desert Air Force, late summer 1942. Flown by P/O. J. L. Waddy. AK846.

3
Mk. III, No. 250 'Sudan' Squadron, No. 239 Wing, RAF, Desert Air Force, El Assa, Tunisia, March 1943. Flown by Fl.-Lt. D. H. Clarke, B Flight Commander. FR313.

4
Mk. III, No. 260 Squadron, No. 233 Wing, RAF, Desert Air Force. FR241.

5
Mk. III, No. 260 Squadron, No. 233 Wing, RAF, Desert Air Force. FR122.

6
Mk. I, No. 112 'Shark' Squadron, No. 239 Wing, RAF, Desert Air Force. AK675.

© WARD

1
Mk. Ia, No. 112 'Shark' Squadron, No. 239 Wing, RAF, Desert Air Force. Serial unknown. Gambut, Libya, March 1942.

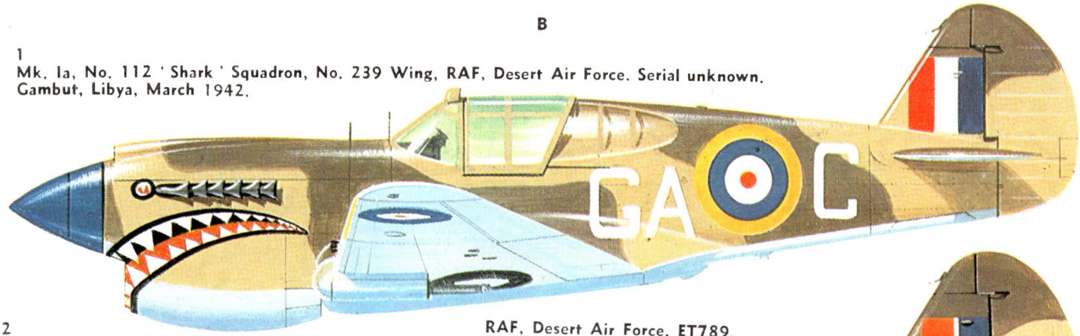

2
Mk. Ia, No. 112 'Shark' Squadron, No. 239 Wing, RAF, Desert Air Force. ET789. LG 91, Amriyha, Egypt, Oct. 1942.

3
Mk. III, No. 112 'Shark' Squadron, No. 239 Wing, RAF, Desert Air Force. FR474. Cutella, Italy, April 1944.

4
Mk. III, No. 112 'Shark' Squadron, No. 239 Wing, RAF, Desert Air Force. Flown by Flt.-Lt. M. N. Matthias. Pachino/Agnone, Sicily, July 1943.

5
Mk. III, No. 112 'Shark' Squadron, Flown by Sqdn.-Ldr. P. F. Illingworth, Squadron OC. FR864. Pachino/Agnone, Sicily, July/Aug. 1943.

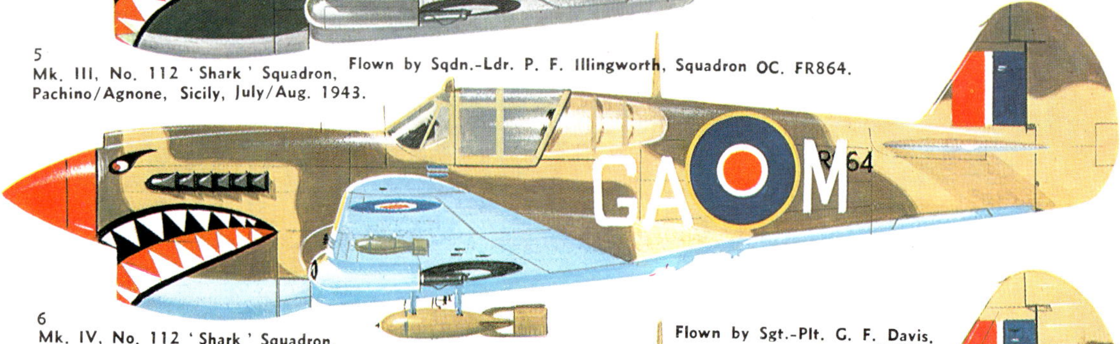

6
Mk. IV, No. 112 'Shark' Squadron, Flown by Sgt.-Plt. G. F. Davis. FX740. Cutella/San Angelo, Italy, March 1944.

1
Mk. Ia, No. 2 'Flying Cheetah' Squadron, SAAF, No. 233 Wing, RAF, Desert Air Force. 1942. Flown by Maj. D. B. Hauptfleisch, AFC, Squadron OC. Serial unknown.

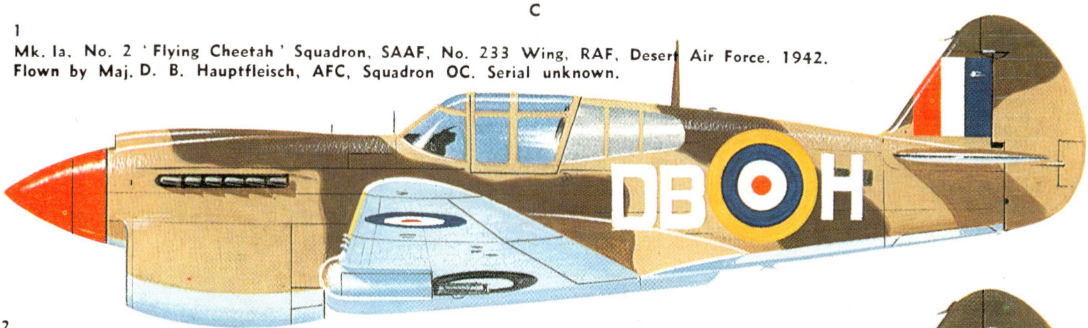

2
Mk. III, No. 2 'Flying Cheetah' Squadron, SAAF, Desert Air Force. 1942. Serial unknown. Flown by Maj. D. B. Hauptfleisch, AFC, Squadron OC.

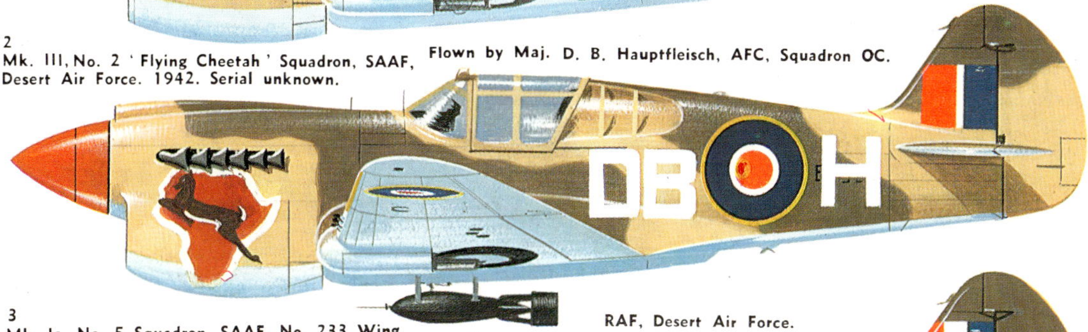

3
Mk. Ia, No. 5 Squadron, SAAF, No. 233 Wing, RAF, Desert Air Force. Serial probably ET961.

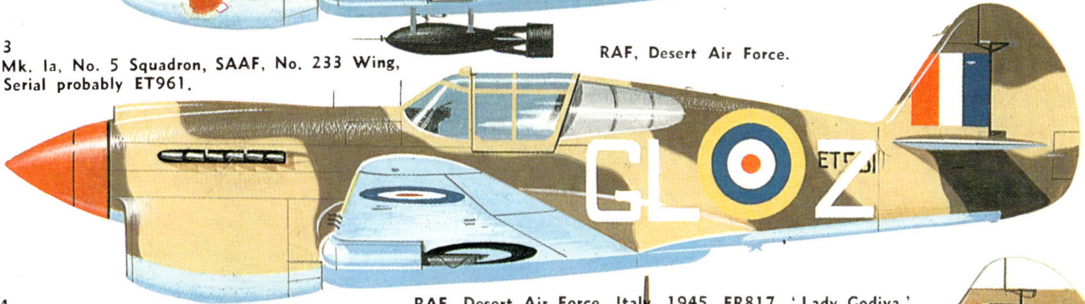

4
Mk. III, No. 5 Squadron, SAAF, No. 233 Wing, RAF, Desert Air Force. Italy, 1945. FR817. 'Lady Godiva'

5
Mk. IV, probably No. 2 OTU Waterkloof, South Africa. SAAF. Serial unknown.

6
Mk. Ia, No. 3 Squadron, RAAF, No. 239 Wing, RAF, Desert Air Force. Serial unknown.

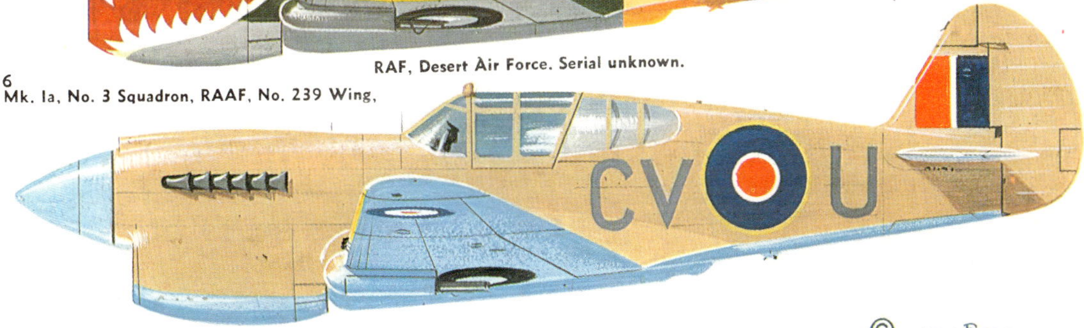

D

1
Mk. Ia, No. 3 Squadron, RAAF, No. 239 Wing, RAF, Desert Air Force, ET953.

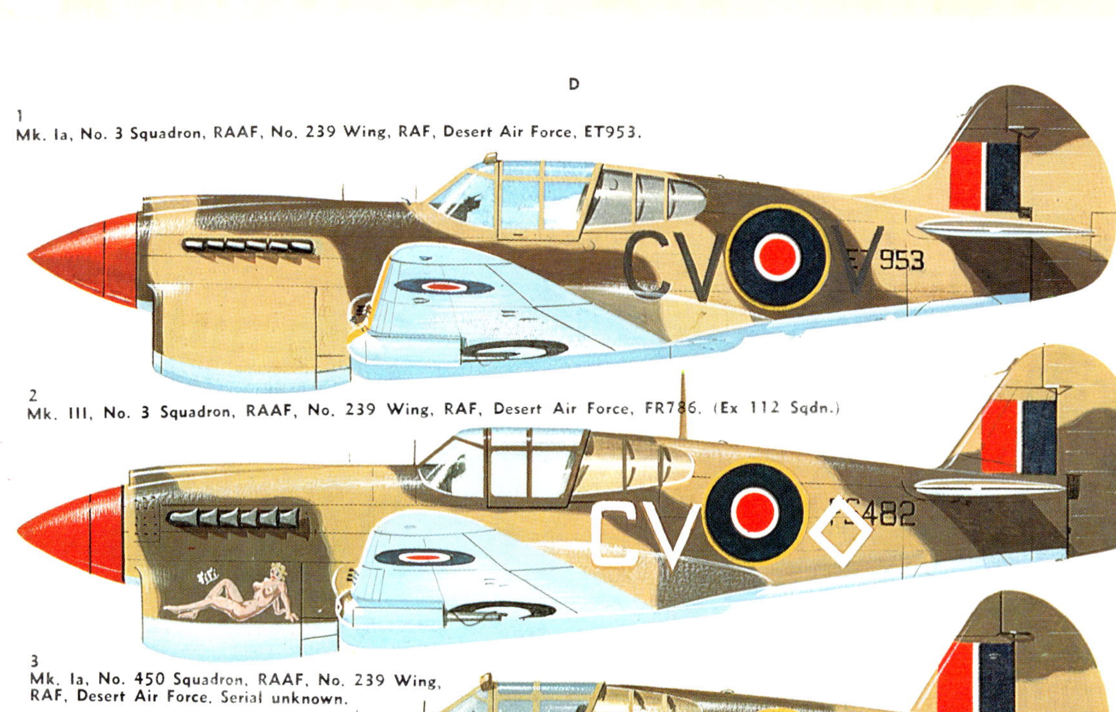

2
Mk. III, No. 3 Squadron, RAAF, No. 239 Wing, RAF, Desert Air Force, FR786. (Ex 112 Sqdn.)

3
Mk. Ia, No. 450 Squadron, RAAF, No. 239 Wing, RAF, Desert Air Force. Serial unknown.

4
Mk. III, No. 450 Squadron, RAAF, No. 239 Wing, RAF, Desert Air Force. FR786.

5
Mk. Ia, of either No. 75 or 76 Squadron, RAAF, Milne Bay, New Guinea, July 1942. Serial unknown.

6
Mk. Ia, No. 1 OTU, RAAF, East Sale, Victoria, Australia. A29-83.

E

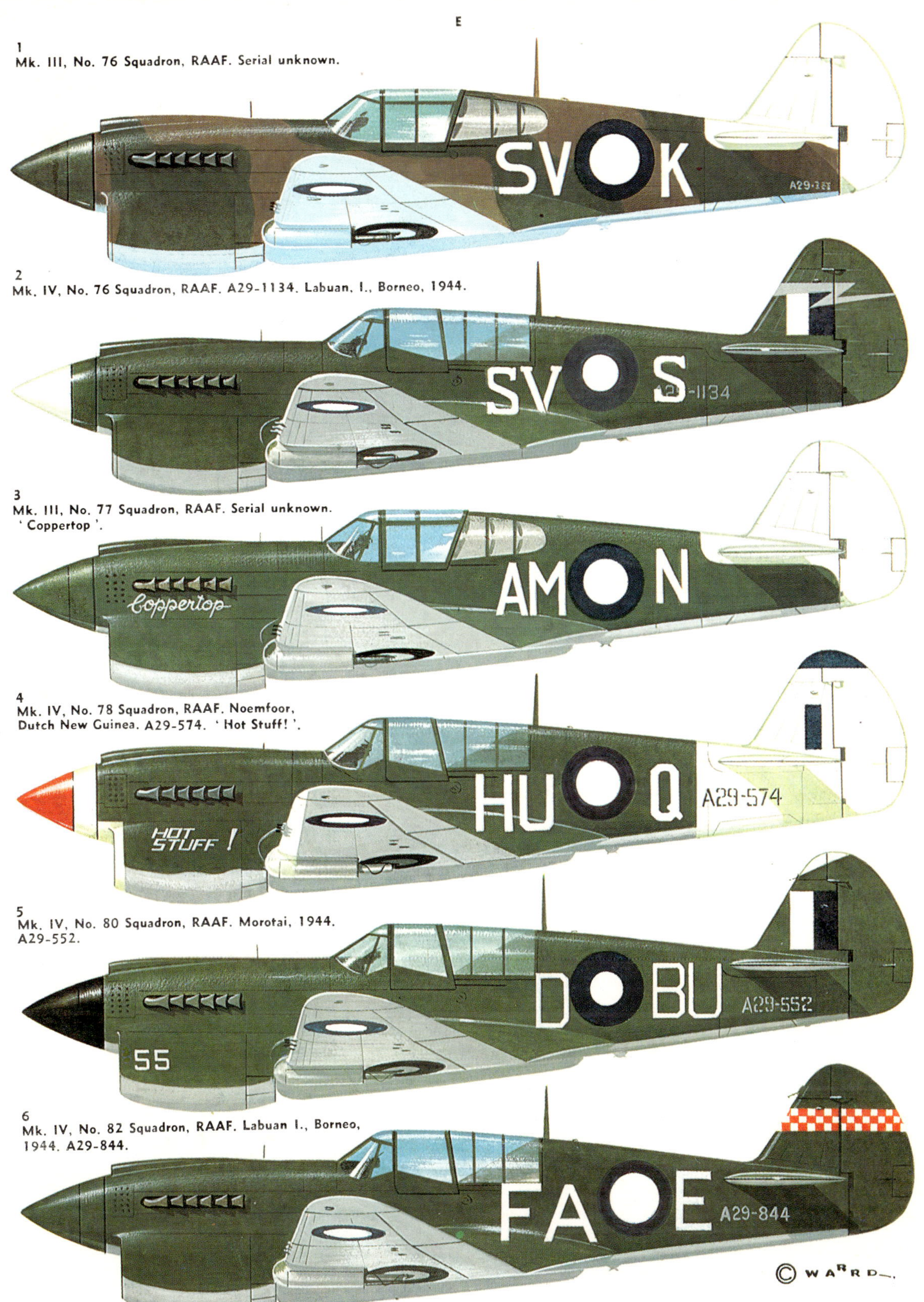

1
Mk. III, No. 76 Squadron, RAAF. Serial unknown.

2
Mk. IV, No. 76 Squadron, RAAF. A29-1134. Labuan, I., Borneo, 1944.

3
Mk. III, No. 77 Squadron, RAAF. Serial unknown. ' Coppertop '.

4
Mk. IV, No. 78 Squadron, RAAF. Noemfoor, Dutch New Guinea. A29-574. ' Hot Stuff! '.

5
Mk. IV, No. 80 Squadron, RAAF. Morotai, 1944. A29-552.

6
Mk. IV, No. 82 Squadron, RAAF. Labuan I., Borneo, 1944. A29-844.

F

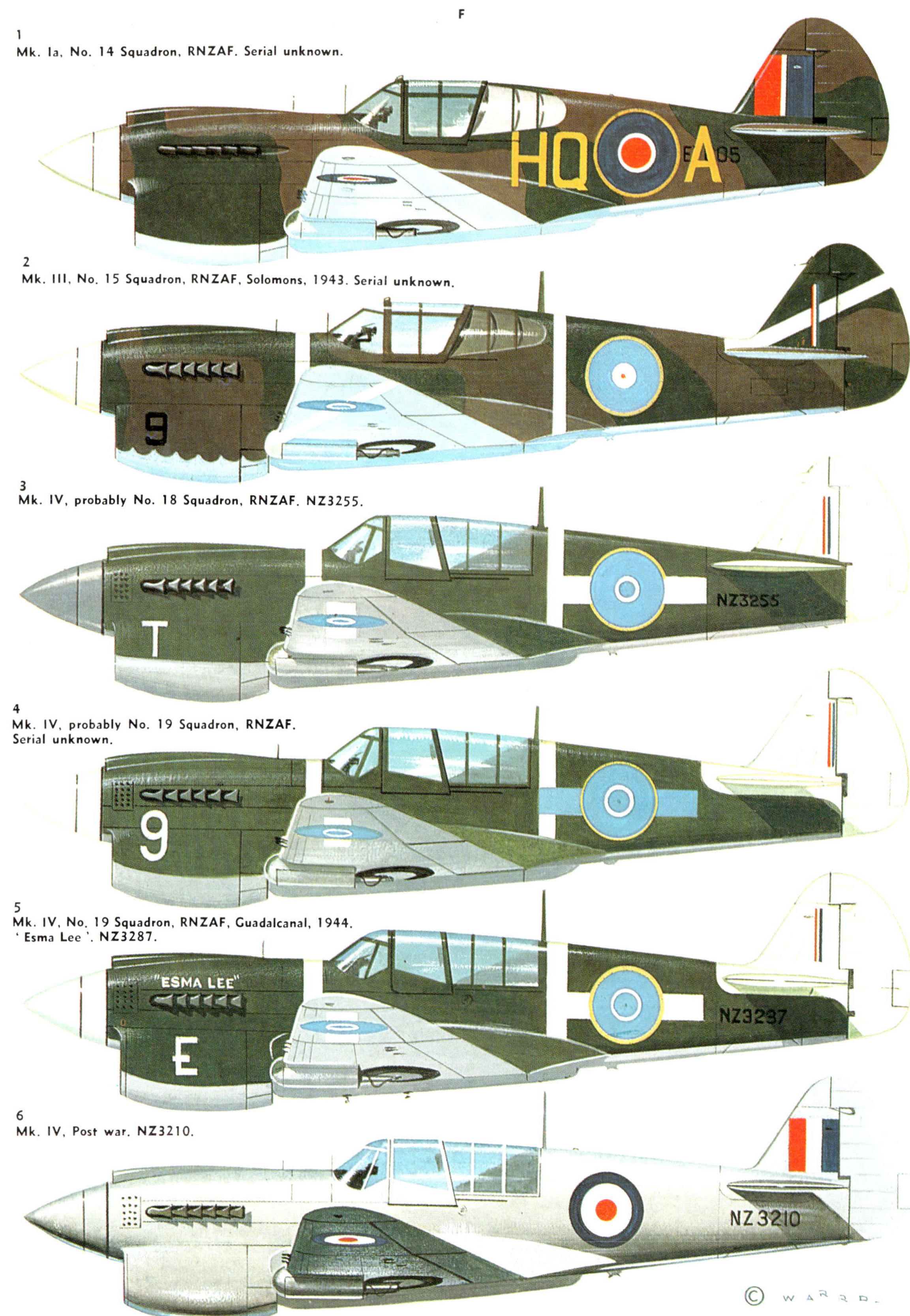

1
Mk. Ia, No. 14 Squadron, RNZAF. Serial unknown.

2
Mk. III, No. 15 Squadron, RNZAF, Solomons, 1943. Serial unknown.

3
Mk. IV, probably No. 18 Squadron, RNZAF. NZ3255.

4
Mk. IV, probably No. 19 Squadron, RNZAF.
Serial unknown.

5
Mk. IV, No. 19 Squadron, RNZAF, Guadalcanal, 1944.
'Esma Lee'. NZ3287.

6
Mk. IV, Post war. NZ3210.

G

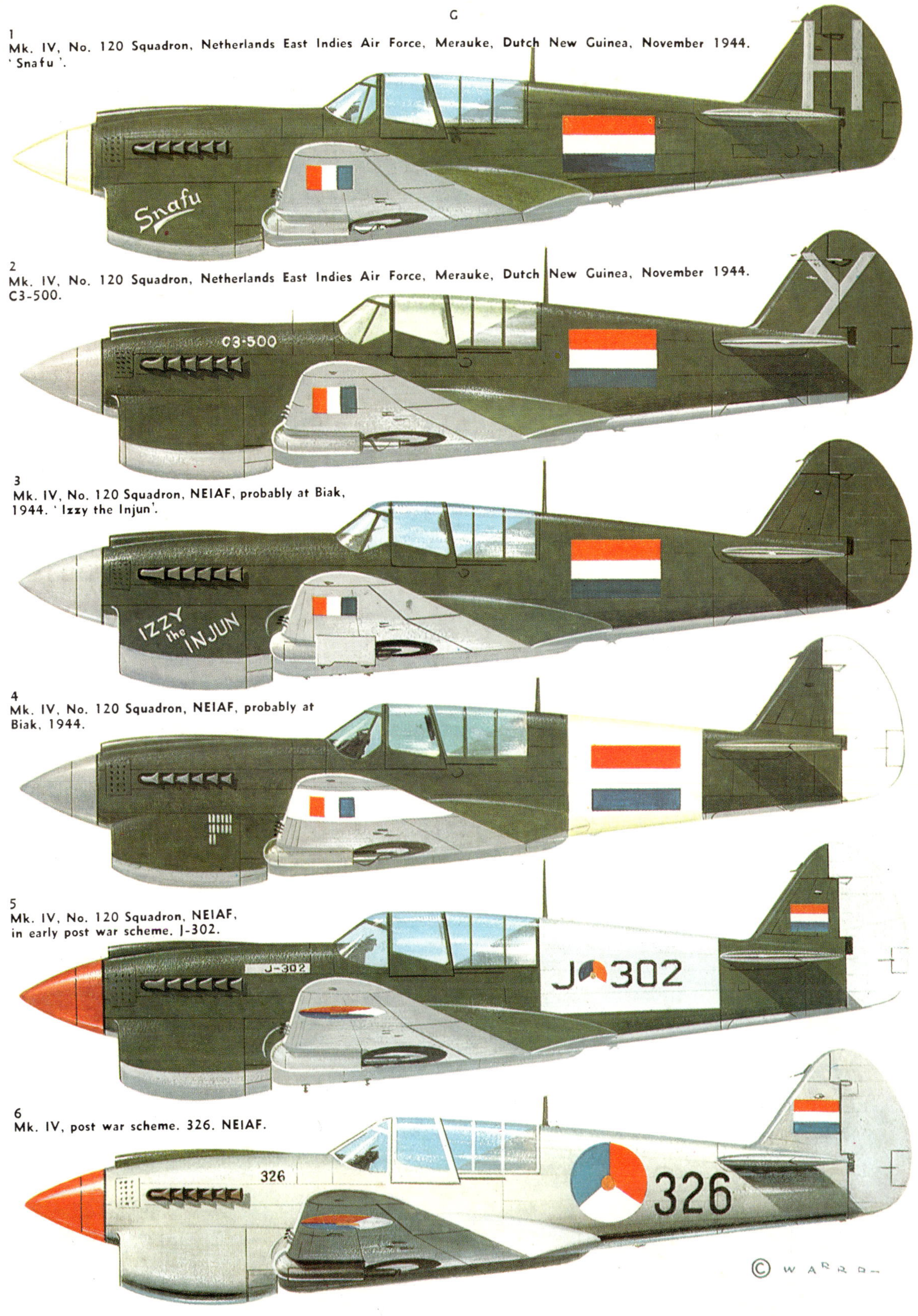

1
Mk. IV, No. 120 Squadron, Netherlands East Indies Air Force, Merauke, Dutch New Guinea, November 1944. 'Snafu'.

2
Mk. IV, No. 120 Squadron, Netherlands East Indies Air Force, Merauke, Dutch New Guinea, November 1944. C3-500.

3
Mk. IV, No. 120 Squadron, NEIAF, probably at Biak, 1944. 'Izzy the Injun'.

4
Mk. IV, No. 120 Squadron, NEIAF, probably at Biak, 1944.

5
Mk. IV, No. 120 Squadron, NEIAF, in early post war scheme. J-302.

6
Mk. IV, post war scheme. 326. NEIAF.

H

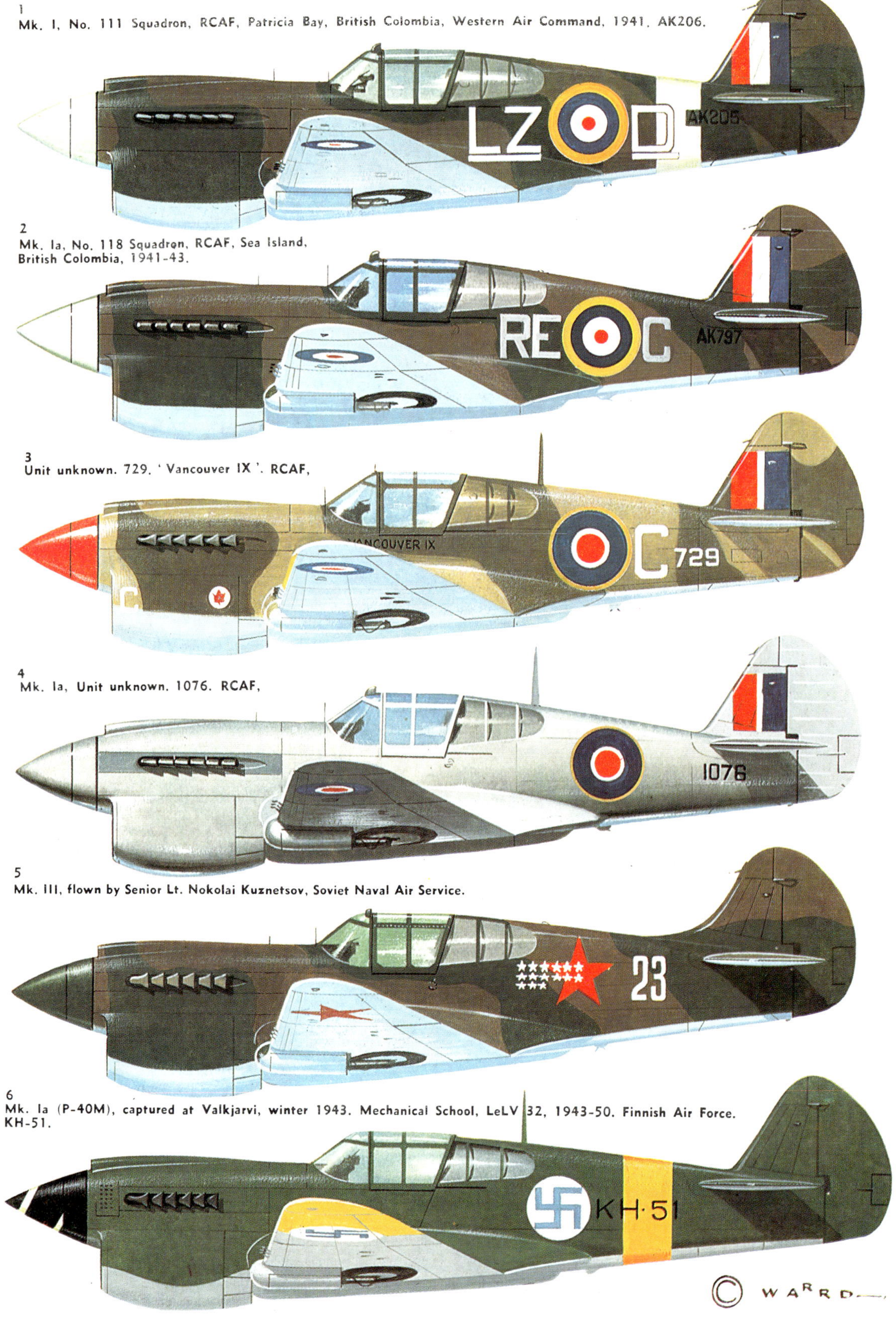

1
Mk. I, No. 111 Squadron, RCAF, Patricia Bay, British Colombia, Western Air Command, 1941. AK206.

2
Mk. Ia, No. 118 Squadron, RCAF, Sea Island, British Colombia, 1941-43.

3
Unit unknown. 729. ' Vancouver IX '. RCAF,

4
Mk. Ia, Unit unknown. 1076. RCAF,

5
Mk. III, flown by Senior Lt. Nokolai Kuznetsov, Soviet Naval Air Service.

6
Mk. Ia (P-40M), captured at Valkjarvi, winter 1943. Mechanical School, LeLV 32, 1943-50. Finnish Air Force. KH-51.

bove Line-up of Mk. IV's of No. 75 Squadron, arakan Island, name on nearest aircraft is)orothy E', serial unknown. OD and grey :heme with white tail units. Note guide Jeep. *(AWM)*

ght & below A29–443 'Gertcha' flown by gt. Geoff. Williams, No. 75 Squadron. Port and arboard views, name on port side only on owl above exhaust ports. *(via Frank F. Smith)*

Below A29–361, SV–Y of No. 76 Squadron, a Mk. III in green/brown and pale blue scheme. *(AWM)*

elow Line-up of Mk. III's, No. 76 quadron RAAF, Kiriwina Strip, riwina Island, Solomon Sea. July 43. Note green/brown uppers le blue unders. *(AWM)*

Left Mk. IV, A29–357 of No. 76 Squ RAAF landing on Vivigani Strip, Gooder Island in the Solomon Sea. 1943.

Above (3 pictures) Mk. IV's of No. 76 Squadron nearest camera with No. 84 Squadron in distance, some aircraft in bare metal finish. Note variations in roundels. *(AWM) Left* Mk. IV with what appears to be 'Sharkmouth' painted on long range tank. *(Right)* SV–B of No. 76 Sqdn. Note white leading edge.

Above Neat line-up of Mk. IV's of No. 78 Squadron on Morotai. Code HU– *(AWM)*

Below Mk. IV's of No. 78 Squadron at Noemfoor, Dutch New Guinea, prior to taking off on a mission against targets on Vogelkop Peninsular, Dutch New Guinea. *(via B. Pattison)*

Above Bare metal Mk. IV of No. 78 Squadron, first allied aircraft to land on Kamiri Strip, Noemfoor. *(AWM)*

Left Line-up of clean and shiny Mk. IV's of No. 80 Squadron, Noemfoor, 10.11. 44. *(via F. Smith)*

Below No. 80 Squadrons dispersal area at Morotai, YMCA truck under nose of 204. *(AWM)*

Above & left Mk. IV's of No. 80 Squadron in dispersal area, Morotai. *(Top AWM; left Peter M. Bowers)*

Mixed formation of Mk. IV's of Nos. 75 & 80 Sqdns

Below Close-up of 'Cleopatra III' flown by Wing Commander G. C. Atherton. *(via B. Pattison)*

& right Neat formation by No. uadron, BU–B in dark green/ scheme, other aircraft in OD/ cheme. BU–B with red tip to r, 'Cleopatra III' in red out- vhite.
otos RAAF via B. Pattison)

Mk. IV's of No. 84 Squadron, .B–. Note variation in size and ns of roundels, all aircraft dark green patches along g and trailing edge of wings ail plane and on fin and on standard USAAF OD/ cheme. LB–K probably A29– *AWM)*

Top No. 82 Squadron dispersal area on Labuan airfield, North Borneo. Note red/white checks on fin and rudder and bare metal Mk. IV coded FA–R in distance. Also note large and small roundels on nearest aircraft. *(AWM)*

Centre Bare metal Mk. IV, No. 82 Squadron, A29–625, code and serial in black. Labuan. *(via d'E. C. Darby)*

Below Bare metal Mk. IV, A29–1193, OD anti-glare panel. Unit unknown. *(via F. Smith)*

Above Neat formation by No. 14 Squadron RNZAF. Mk. Ia's in green/brown uppers, pale blue unders. Name on cowl of HQ–B 'Umslopogaas' with small lightning flash, all in white. *(via d'E. C. Darby)*

Right Stepped down formation by No. 15 Squadron, RNZAF. JZ–I NZ.3040. Green/brown uppers, pale blue unders. *(RNZAF)*

Below Line-up of Mk. Ia's of No. 15 Squadron, RNZAF. JZ–P NZ.3037. Whenuapai. *(New Zealand Herald via d'E. C. Darby)*

Below Magnificient shot of Mk. Ia's of No. 16 Squadron, RNZAF. Note red/white/blue roundels. XO–M NZ.3029. *(RNZAF)*

Above & left Mk. IV's on a New Z-
land airfield ready to fly out to
islands, note Hudsons in backgrou
(Both photos IW

Above With a Hudson acting as navigator Mk. IV's head out over the sea for the islands. OD and grey scheme, red/white/blue roundels on fuselage. *(*

Below Mk. III's of No. 15 Squadron, RNZAF, Solomons, 1943. Green/brown uppers, pale blue unders. *(IWM)*

Above Neat formation of Mk. IV's of an unknown squadron. Blue/white/blue roundels. OD and grey scheme. Squadron may be No. 18 *(RNZAF)*

Right Mk. IV taxying along runway, Torokina airfield, Bougainville Island. *(USN)*

Left Poor photograph, but apart from the combat damage, interesting as it shows the tiny red centre in the roundel. *(d'E. C. Darby)*

Below Vic of Mk. IV's of an unknown squadron taking off. Red/white/blue roundels. *(via d'E. C. Darby)*

Mk. IV Flown by P/O A. A. Watson, No. 19 Squadron, RNZAF, Guadalcanal, 1944, NZ 3287, see colour illustration 'ESNA LEE'
(d'E. C. Darby)

NZ 3119, Mk. III in OD and grey finish, note blue/white/blue under wing roundel.
(via R. C. Jones)

Mk. IV No. 4 Fighter Operational Training Unit. NZ 3256 in stencil style. Very faded OD and grey scheme, red/white spinner and red roundel centres. Pale blue code.

Another Mk. IV of No. 4, SOTU in faded OD and grey, note OD showing through white rudder. NZ 3246,
(via R. C. Jones)

This Mk. III appears to be NZ 3119 stripped down to bare metal with black spinner and anti-glare panel.
(via R. C. Jones)

Above Mk. Ia's of No. 111 Squadron, RCAF, Western Air Command, squadron operated from Sea Island, Patricia Bay, B.C., and Anchorage, Alaska. LZ–code used 11–41 to 12–43. *(IWM)*

Below (3 pictures) Mk. Ia's of No. 118 Squadron, RCAF. Wheel disc on RE–C blue/white outlined red. *(Photos RCAF)*

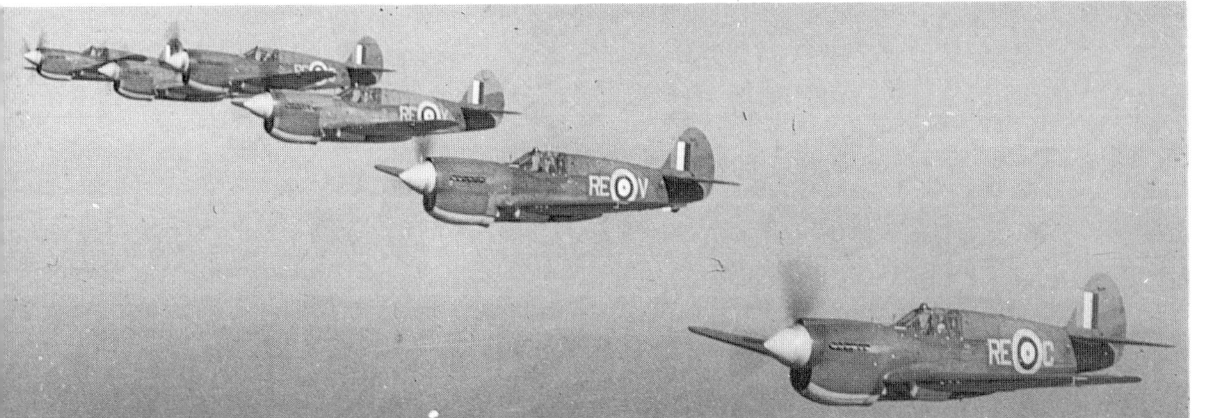

Above Mk. Ia in standard green/brown uppers, pale blue unders. Note red/white/blue roundels on wings. Photo probably taken after Oct. 1942 when sqdn. codes were discontinued for security reasons.

Above Mk. Ia, serial unknown, taking off from Patricia Bay.

Above Line-up of Mk. Ia's being refuelled at Patricia Bay, 20.11.42. Aircraft nearest camera AK 905.

Below Mk. Ia showing something of a contrast. RAF standard desert scheme over the snows of Canada. Serial ET611. *(All photos RCAF)*

Left Mk. Ia, 'Vancouver IX' C 729. See colour illustration for port side details. RCAF. *(Peter M. Bowers)*

Right Mk. Ia, 1009. Black F aft of roundel port and stbd. RCAF. *(via D. W. Menard)*

Below left Mk. Ia, 1073 in RAF desert scheme. *(Peter M. Bowers)*

Below right Mk. Ia, serial unknown with black PN on cowl. This particular Kittyhawk survived the war and is presently being restored by G. A. Maude. *(G. A. Maude)*

ght Mk. IV, 867, in bare metal finish, OD anti-re panel and fin. See cover illustration. Unit known. *(Peter M. Bowers)*

low Mk. Ia in bare metal finish, 1076 in black. *(RCAF)*

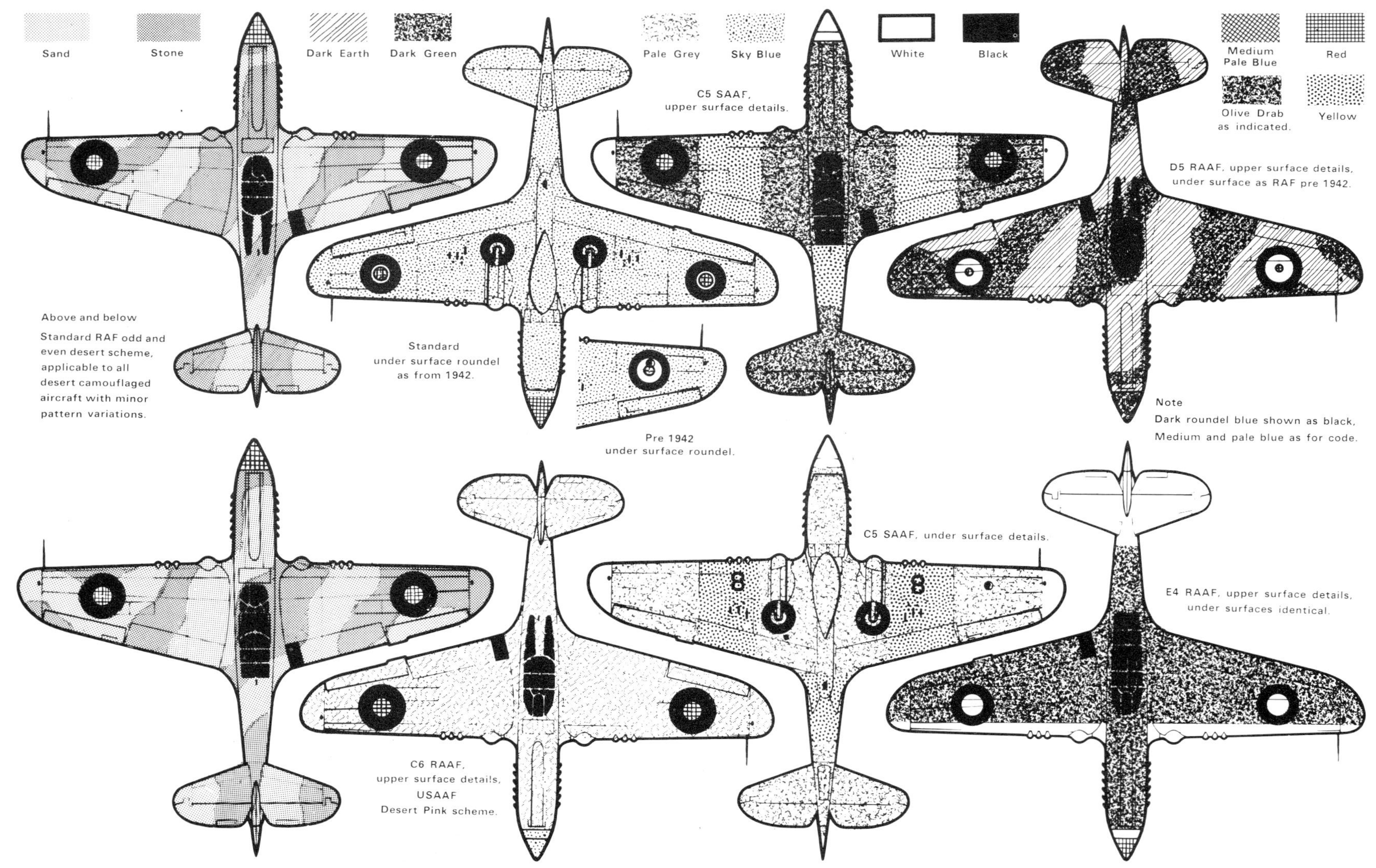
Sand
Stone
Dark Earth
Dark Green
Pale Grey
Sky Blue
White
Black
Medium Pale Blue
Red
Olive Drab as indicated.
Yellow
Above and below Standard RAF odd and even desert scheme, applicable to all desert camouflaged aircraft with minor pattern variations.
Standard under surface roundel as from 1942.
C5 SAAF, upper surface details.
Pre 1942 under surface roundel.
D5 RAAF, upper surface details, under surface as RAF pre 1942.
Note
Dark roundel blue shown as black, Medium and pale blue as for code.
C6 RAAF, upper surface details, USAAF Desert Pink scheme.
C5 SAAF, under surface details.
E4 RAAF, upper surface details, under surfaces identical.

Bottom, inside front cover, upper surface details, dark green on OD. Mk. IV, No. 84 Sqdn. RAAF.
F/O G. B. Fisken's aircraft, see front cover. Roundels pale blue/white/pale blue on wings, red/white/pale blue/ yellow on fuselage
All stripes are thinly outlined with dark red. Black 19 port and stbd.
G1,2,3 Upper surface details, under surfaces identical. No. 120 Sqdn. NEIAF.
Personal insignia and score markings on Fisken's a/c. Black cat outlined white, white 'Wairaapa Wildcat', white Jap flag with red details.
19
Wairarapa Wildcat
G4 Upper surface details, under surfaces identical. No. 120 Sqdn. NEIAF.
Fourth down, inside front cover, upper surface details, under surface roundel as upper. Mk. Ia, No. 16 Sqdn. RNZAF
F3,4,5 upper surface details, all roundels pale blue/white/pale blue, fuselage with yellow outer ring. Under surfaces identical.
G6 Mk. IV, NEIAF post war. Orange centre to roundel, under surfaces identical.
H6 KH51, Finnish AF. Upper surface details, below under surface detail showing yellow outer wing. Pale blue swastika on white disc.

Nice shot of four Mk. IV's of No. 120 Squadron, Netherlands East Indies Air Force. See colour illustration. Letters on fin and rudder originally white *(via G. H. Kamphuis)*

Mk. IV of No. 120 Squadron NEIAF on Merauke airfield, Dutch New Guinea. Note serial C3-503, stencil style, repeated on drop tank.

Mk. IV's revving up in dispersal area at Merauke. At the time this photo was taken letters had only recently been painted on fin and rudders in white. *(G. H Kamphuis)*